# BENEATH THE CROSS

# Beneath the Cross

## Meditations on the Seven Last Words

### THE MOST REVEREND
### Gerardo J. Colacicco

FIRST EDITION

*Jubilee Studio 33*

CLINTON CORNERS, NEW YORK

BENEATH THE CROSS
*Meditations on the Seven Last Words*

*Nihil Obstat:*   Reverend Matthew S. Ernest, STD
Reverend Kevin J. O'Reilly, STD
*Censores Librorum*

*Imprimatur:*   Reverend Monsignor Joseph P. LaMorte, VG
*Vicar General, Archdiocese of New York*
October 22, 2020

JUBILEE STUDIO 33 is an imprint of The Attic Studio Publishing House
P.O. Box 75 • Clinton Corners, NY 12514 • Phone: 845-266-8100
JubileeStudio33@aol.com          •          AtticStudioPress@aol.com

PRINTED IN THE UNITED STATES OF AMERICA   5 4 3 2 1

Quantity discounts of *BENEATH THE CROSS* are available from the publisher on bulk purchases for parishes, schools, church groups, etc. For further information please email **beneaththecross7@gmail.com** or call **845-266-8100**. *Thank you.*

ISBN–13:  978-1-883551-82-7
ISBN–10:  1-883551-82-X

Library of Congress Control Number: 2020953041

DEDICATED

to

*Our Lady*

*Iuxta Crucem tecum stare*

Beneath the Cross with you to stay

– Stabat Mater

# ST. PATRICK'S CATHEDRAL

## "America's Parish Church"

### NEW YORK CITY

The meditations contained in this book were
first preached at St. Patrick's Cathedral
by Bishop Gerardo Colacicco on

## GOOD FRIDAY
## APRIL 10, 2020

# CONTENTS

# FOREWORD

THE LEGENDARY Archbishop Fulton J. Sheen called it, "the most effective pulpit ever." He meant the pulpit of the Cross on a hill called Calvary on a Friday strangely called good, preached by One — true God and true man — as He suffered three hours of torment.

From that ambo, He uttered seven sentences, which a tearful history now calls His Seven Last Words. His congregation that day was small: His own mother and beloved disciple, some jeering Roman soldiers, a crook on either side, masochistic gawkers passing by... and then millions through the millennia who pause annually on that Friday and ponder them again in packed churches, able to answer "yes" to the question, "Were you there when they crucified my Lord?"

As that hill outside Jerusalem in 33 A.D. was called a crossroads, so is St. Patrick's Cathedral on Fifth Avenue in the heart of what Pope St. John Paul II termed "the capital of the world" — New York City. Pope Francis looked with awe upon it and observed, "It's right in the middle of it all."

For over a century, thousands have packed St. Patrick's to hear a preacher re-create the drama of Calvary and lead His disciples of the day in reflecting upon those classic Seven Last Words. Television and radio — and now livestream — carry the meditations all over the world.

And so on Good Friday, April 10, 2020, did a brand new bishop, one Gerardo Colacicco, climb the famed pulpit to deliver his meditations. Highly regarded as a sincere, effective preacher by generations of his own parishioners, he confessed awe at the place, the words, and the

11

task, but came through in the tradition of Archbishop Fulton Sheen, Bishop Robert Barron, and John Cardinal O'Connor. His celebrated humility did not, thank God, keep him from an invitation to have his poetic meditations published . . . and here they are!

Usually, I admit, in one way "you have to be there" to watch the people listen, cry, smile — people from all over the world, who seek sanctuary in those haunting *Tre Ore (Three Hours)* in "America's parish church," St. Patrick's Cathedral.

Not Good Friday 2020. A new version of the Passion had gripped the world, this one called COVID-19. Millions that year depended upon the

airwaves, since "the doors were locked, for fear of" . . . *the virus.* But the suffering of Jesus resonated more than ever with a city, a nation, a planet, afraid, alone, infected.

And, thanks to Bishop Colacicco, we all came away closer to Jesus. The gospel episodes of those who encountered Jesus, skillfully preached by the bishop, coaxed us all to feel like a friend of the One on the Cross. That— friendship with Jesus—as Pope Benedict XVI claimed, brought us holiness, in a week called holy, on a day called good, when the earth quaked with sadness and the sun hid in shame.

*"We adore Thee, O Christ, and we praise Thee! Because by Thy Holy Cross Thou hast redeemed the world!"*

And we thank you, Bishop Colacicco, for bringing us closer to the wood of the Cross, the *spes unica,* our unparalleled source of hope, at a time we sure needed it!

† Timothy Michael Cardinal Dolan
Archbishop of New York

# INTRODUCTION

THROUGHOUT THE GOSPELS, we encounter people whom Jesus engaged through His preaching, teaching, and healing. Some of these encounters are brief and we never hear from these individuals again; we assume that when they left Jesus' presence, they went on living their lives differently than they had before.

Have you ever wondered what happened to them? Did their paths ever cross again? Is it so far beyond our spiritual imagination to consider that they might have gathered at the foot of the Cross on that Friday we call good? If Our Divine Lord had fulfilled a need in their lives — if He had forgiven, challenged, healed, resuscitated, even celebrated with them—might they in turn have come to Him in His time of need?

We often focus our attention and meditation on the spiritual and theological significance of His last words upon the Cross. On this Good Friday, let us hear His words spoken and heard through the perspectives of those very individuals whom He encountered during His public ministry. Those people who, very much like ourselves, came to know, love, and believe in Jesus during challenging times in their lives.

How did they hear His last words? We know that many Jews came to Jerusalem to observe the Passover. Couldn't these individuals have been among those gathered to celebrate the feast? Couldn't they have learned the news of Our Lord's trial and the verdict of crucifixion and felt the need to seek Him out and be with Him in His time of need?

Let us enter into this time of prayer with those who are very familiar to us. Let us imagine, if you will, that they make their way to Calvary, only to hear a word that strikes a memory of the encounter — an encounter that not only changed their lives, but also revealed to the world who it is who once walked among us preaching, teaching, and healing, and now hangs upon the Cross for our salvation.

# THE FIRST WORD

And when they came to the place which is called The Skull, there they crucified him, and the criminals, one on the right and one on the left. And Jesus said, **"Father, forgive them; for they know not what they do."**

*Luke 23:33-34a*

# The Woman Caught in Adultery

*John 8:2-11*

FROM THE GOSPEL ACCORDING TO ST. JOHN:

*The scribes and the Pharisees brought
a woman who had been caught in adultery,
and placing her in their midst they said to [Jesus],
"Teacher, this woman has been caught in the
act of adultery. Now in the law Moses commanded
us to stone such. What do you say about her?"
This they said to test him, that they
might have some charge to bring
against him.* – John 8:3-6a

WHEN I CAME INTO THE WORLD, my mother died in childbirth. Because of that, my father always resented me. I never felt his love, so I lived my life trying to fill that void. I loved every man who paid any attention to me, trying desperately to make up for the love I never had.

I met You, Jesus, under the most embarrassing of circumstances and I was so ashamed. I had heard about You, but I didn't pay You much mind — until I found myself thrown on the ground at Your feet. I was caught. They caught me — and this man I didn't even know — in adultery. How did I know he was married? I didn't even care if he was or wasn't. I just wanted someone to love me.

I thought that this was the end. They all had rocks and they were aimed at me. But You remained calm. You began to write with Your finger on the ground. The sand began to reveal words: *pride, envy, anger, sloth, gluttony, avarice, lust.* I will never forget them; they were etched into my memory as You wrote them on the ground. Then You said to them, "Let him who is without sin among you be the first to throw a stone at her."

I held my breath and braced myself for the first blow. You began to write on the ground again: *mercy, forgiveness…* I closed my eyes and saw nothing more. I waited for the worst… but instead heard the thump of one stone after another falling to the ground.

Soon they had all disappeared. There was no one left but You and me. I held my breath, wondering what You were going to say or do to me. Then calmly and gently You asked me where they all were. "Has no one condemned you?"

With my voice shaking I simply replied, "No one, Lord."

Then I heard the words that I waited all my life to hear, "Neither do I condemn you; go, and do not sin again." Finally, love — real love — the love that I was searching for my entire life. Everything became clear at that moment. I didn't realize what I was doing with my life. I had no idea until You calmly spoke those words to me. It all made sense, only because of Your compassion.

Now I am once again on the ground at Your feet, clinging to Your Cross. I hear You speak, *"Father, forgive them; for they know not what they do."* Even nailed to the Cross, You have this amazing capacity to forgive. I didn't know what I was doing all those years, but You knew. You understood what I didn't.

Now they turn on You with the same fury with which they were determined to destroy me. But sadly, instead of the sound of stones falling to the ground, I hear the sound of the nails being driven into Your hands and feet. Mercy and forgiveness are no longer written on the ground but are spoken from Your lips. I will not leave this spot for as long as You hang here. I will cling to the foot of Your Cross for as long as it takes.

# The Rich Young Man

### Matthew 19:16-22

FROM THE GOSPEL ACCORDING TO ST. MATTHEW:

*And behold, one came up to [Jesus], saying, "Teacher,*
*what good deed must I do, to have eternal life?" And*
*he said to him, "Why do you ask me about what is good?*
*One there is who is good. If you would enter life, keep*
*the commandments." He said to him, "Which?"*
*And Jesus said, "You shall not kill, You shall not commit*
*adultery, You shall not steal, You shall not bear false*
*witness, Honor your father and mother, and, You shall*
*love your neighbor as yourself." The young man said to*
*him, "All these I have observed; what do I still lack?"*
*Jesus said to him, "If you would be perfect, go, sell what*
*you possess and give to the poor, and you will have*
*treasure in heaven; and come, follow me." When the*
*young man heard this he went away sorrowful;*
*for he had great possessions. – Matthew 19:16-22*

I WAS INTRIGUED BY YOU, but I can now admit that I thought more highly of myself. I knew the law and was somewhat proud of my observance of it. My family was wealthy and I enjoyed the respect our wealth received from the people of our region.

I heard about You, Jesus. I was curious. I devised a question whose answer would not reveal Your wisdom as much as it would reveal my pride. You engaged me and we went back and forth. Throughout our conversation, You looked at me in a way that made me very uncomfortable. It felt as if You were looking into my very soul—like You knew me—better than I thought I knew myself. Intrigue was replaced with respect; pride was turned to embarrassment.

Something strange was happening to me while we spoke; something I never experienced before. I was almost brought to tears but fought with every ounce of my strength to control myself. I asked You what I lacked, and Your words burned themselves on my mind and soul. You said to me, "If you would be perfect, go, sell what you possess and give to the poor, and you will have treasure in heaven; and come, follow Me."

First, I thought I was already near perfect. The fact that You used that word stung me to the core because You were letting me know that I was not. Sell what I possess? Never in a million years would the thought of doing such a thing enter my mind. It would be an impossibility. How would I live? What would my family say? What of my position in our village? There was too much to risk, too much at stake. Sell everything…it's madness, just madness. Then the final blow, "Come, follow Me." Part of me wanted to, but the other part of me was stronger.

Sorrowfully, I walked away. I didn't know what else to do. I was disappointed in myself—embarrassed, ashamed. I walked away and I've regretted doing so all this time. Yet, despite the regret, I still can't leave behind everything that defines who I am. My possessions own me rather than the other way around.

But now is the moment of truth. I heard what was happening to You here in Jerusalem so I came. I'm not sure why I came. I am just here. I see You stripped of everything. They nail You nearly naked to the cross.

No possessions here, yet everything is now accomplished. You once asked me if I wanted to be perfect. Now perfection is revealed in the ability to forgive.

Forgive me, Lord, for not letting go of my wealth. Forgive me for not having the courage to follow You. Forgive me, Lord, because it is only now on this hill of Calvary that I realize what I turned my back on.

I thought I went away sorrowful after our first meeting. That was nothing compared to the sorrow I now feel in the very depth of my heart. *Father, forgive them; for they know not what they do.* Those words are not only directed towards those who physically nailed You to the Cross today, but I can swear that when You say these words You look at me. I had no idea who and what I walked away from then. But I am here now. I hope I am not too late. Please, Lord, may I not be too late.

# THE SECOND WORD

One of the criminals who were hanged railed at him, saying, "Are you not the Christ? Save yourself and us!" But the other rebuked him, saying, "Do you not fear God, since you are under the same sentence of condemnation? And we indeed justly; for we are receiving the due reward of our deeds; but this man has done nothing wrong." And he said, "Jesus, remember me when you come in your kingly power." And he said to him, **"Truly, I say to you, today you will be with me in Paradise."**

*Luke 23:39-43*

# *The Paralytic Lowered from the Roof*

### *Mark 2:1-12*

FROM THE GOSPEL ACCORDING TO ST. MARK:

*And when [Jesus] returned to Caper'na-um after some days, it was reported that he was at home. And many were gathered together, so that there was no longer room for them, not even about the door; and he was preaching the word to them. And they came, bringing to him a paralytic carried by four men.* – Mark 2:1-3

FOR A GOOD PERIOD OF MY LIFE I could not walk. The doctors told my parents that I had some disease; others were of the mind that my affliction was the result of some sin, some transgression of the law. All I knew from my youth was that I could not walk. I was dependent upon my family and friends to get me from one place to another. At times, I felt that I was a nuisance. Other times, I just resigned myself to waiting. I was not always patient...especially with myself.

One evening, my friends came over to visit. They were discussing You. What they were saying seemed amazing, beyond possibility. They said that You could heal. They said that there were stories about miracles and cures, and they were really intrigued. I never heard them talk like this before and I began to daydream about...possibilities.

21

Whenever they came over to visit, I would ask for more news. What else have you heard about Him? What else has He done? One evening they said You talked about a kingdom, but they weren't quite sure what that all meant. Their focus was always that You could heal.

Then the day arrived—a day that started out like any other but ended up changing my life forever.

My friends came running into the house all excited, so out of breath they could hardly speak. They told me that You were in my village. They wanted to take me to You. They lifted me onto my mat and began to run to where You were. I was so frightened because they were going so fast I thought they were going to drop me.

A huge crowd surrounded a house. They said You were inside, but we couldn't even get close to the door. No one was moving to let us through. They laid me on the ground and said that eventually You would have to come out, and that when You did, then they would bring You to me. We sat there for what seemed an eternity, but You didn't come out.

One of my friends went off. He walked around the crowd to the back of the house. He was gone for a while. When he returned, he called my other friends over and they were talking. Finally, they came to me and said that the back of the house was clear and that my friend had found a ladder.

They wanted to bring me up on the roof and lower me down. I told them they were out of their minds. What if they dropped me? What would the owner of the house say? I began to list all the reasons why this was not a good idea. Then finally they said to me, "Do you want to walk again?" "Yes," I said. "Do you believe that Jesus can heal you?" "Yes," I said. "Then let's go."

They picked me up and off we went. I was nervous, scared but at the same time excited and hopeful.

We made it up onto the roof, then they began to open it up and lower me down. There You were, teaching. You stood up and helped lower me to the floor along with the assistance of some others. I will never forget what

You said. I will never forget what You did. I believed that You could heal me, and You did.

For the first time in my life, I was able to walk.

Little did I know that my footsteps would bring me here to Calvary. I almost wish that I couldn't walk up that hill, but I would go anywhere to be with You, especially now. I hear the thief taunt You. "Come down," he says.

Come down. I think of how I was lowered down from the roof. But You don't come down. I hear the other thief say, "Remember me when You come into Your Kingdom," and I remembered the conversations with my friends about this Kingdom. Then I hear You say, *Today you will be with Me in Paradise.* It only takes a day, I think to myself, for one's whole life to change. One day, that's all. And Paradise? Is that the Kingdom? Is the Kingdom Paradise?

All I know is that I couldn't walk but now I can. That on my own I was able to walk up this hill to stand beneath Your cross. That I, too, want to be part of this Kingdom. I, too, want to be with You in Paradise. Until now, "paradise" was being able to walk. Paradise was being able to get to one place or another whenever I wanted to go, not having to wait for anyone else to bring me. Yet now there is another place to go, and only You can bring me, and I want to go.

Carry me once more, Jesus. Bring me to Your Kingdom. Bring me to Paradise. You made it possible for me to walk; now I see that You make it possible for me and others to have a place to go.

# THE THIRD WORD

But standing by the cross of Jesus were his mother, and his mother's sister, Mary the wife of Clopas, and Mary Mag'dalene. When Jesus saw his mother, and the disciple whom he loved standing near, he said to his mother, **"Woman, behold, your son!"** Then he said to the disciple, **"Behold, your mother!"** And from that hour the disciple took her to his own home.

*John 19:25b-27*

# The Raising of the Widow's Son

*Luke 7:11-17*

FROM THE GOSPEL ACCORDING TO ST. LUKE:

*Soon afterward [Jesus] went to a city called Na'in,
and his disciples and a great crowd went with him.
As he drew near to the gate of the city, behold, a man
who had died was being carried out, the only son of
his mother, and she was a widow; and a large crowd
from the city was with her.* – Luke 7:11-12

WORD SPREAD QUICKLY in our village of Nain. They said that You were arrested and brought to trial. They said that it didn't sound good for You and that there was a strong possibility that things would go badly for You. We packed a few of our things and got here as soon as we could. We wanted to be with You when You needed us most. It is a small way to give back to You who were certainly with us at the time we most needed You.

I lost my husband years ago. Thank God I had my son. He took care of me, he protected me, and he made sure that I had whatever I needed. Then suddenly, he died. There was no warning, no illness, nothing... just here one day and gone the next. I was devastated. What would happen now? My grief was so strong that I couldn't sleep, I couldn't eat, I could hardly walk behind my son as we took him to his grave. The people of my town held me up; each step was agony.

Then this stranger came.

They told me You stood for a short time off in the distance and just watched me. You were obviously moved by my loss and my grief. You came closer and stopped the procession. I will never forget what happened next.

You spoke and my son came back to life. I was so shocked that I nearly fainted. You gave him back to me. You whispered in my ear, "Mother, behold, your son."

Here You say those very words again. *Behold, your son.* I am amazed that You say them now, from the Cross. This time, not to me but to Your own mother. I look at her and remember how I felt. My heart breaks for her. I know her heart is breaking because mine was broken. I want to hold her tight and let her know that if You could give me my son back, You will make sure to take care of her, too.

Then I hear You say, "*Behold, your mother.*" A young man goes to her and puts his arm around her. I ask who he is and am told his name is John. My heart skips a beat because that is my son's name as well. *Behold, your son. Behold, your mother.* I can't help but think what these relationships mean now, as we stand at the foot of Your Cross.

Everything is different now. You, Jesus, on the Cross change everything, even our relationships. *My* John isn't really *my* John at all; he is every mother's son. And am I everyone's mother? That's what You do, Jesus. If we belong to You, then we belong to each other.

3B

## *Our Lady's Meditation*

*Luke 2:22-40*

FROM THE GOSPEL ACCORDING TO ST. LUKE:

*And his father and his mother marveled*
*at what was said about him; and Simeon*
*blessed them and said to Mary his mother,*
*"Behold, this child is set for the fall and rising of*
*many in Israel, and for a sign that is spoken against*
*(and a sword will pierce through your own soul also),*
*that thoughts out of many hearts may be revealed."*
– Luke 2:33-35

STANDING HERE makes me think of the day Joseph and I took You to the temple to fulfill the law. I held You in my arms, while Simeon offered the prescribed prayers. Then he took You from me and, while You were in the arms of this venerable old man, he looked at me and said words that I have never forgotten: *a sword would pierce my heart.* This is what he meant; this moment is what he foretold. I could never have imagined this moment. Never!

Now You look at me as You looked at me while in Simeon's arms. I felt helpless then and I feel even more helpless now. In the midst of Your agony, You are still taking care of Your mother — watching out for me, making sure I will be taken care of, fulfilling the promise You made to Joseph while we both sat by his bedside before he died. "Take care of Your mother for me," he said. You looked at me then as well, with tears in Your eyes. I thought You were crying for Joseph, but now I wonder, were those tears because You knew this moment would come to pass? I treasure the times our eyes caught sight of each other throughout Your life. No words, just that penetrating glance that I had gotten used to but often didn't fully understand.

Here in the midst of this horror, I can't take my eyes off of You. This time You speak, *"Behold, your son."* I have never stopped beholding You and I never will. You give me John to make sure I am cared for. We will help each other; we will take care of each other. I promise. The pain in my heart is so intense, I don't think I can bear it.

I feel John's arm around me and I bury myself in his chest and weep.

*"... standing near the cross of Jesus
were his mother... and the disciple
whom he loved."* – John 19:25, 26

# THE FOURTH WORD

Now from the sixth hour there was darkness over all the land until the ninth hour. And about the ninth hour Jesus cried with a loud voice, "Eli, Eli, la'ma sabach-tha'ni?" that is, **"My God, my God, why have you forsaken me?"**

*Matthew 27:45-46*

# The Blind Man
## at the Side of the Road

*Luke 18:35-43*

FROM THE GOSPEL ACCORDING TO ST. LUKE:

*As [Jesus] drew near to Jericho, a blind man was sitting by the roadside begging; and hearing a multitude going by, he inquired what this meant. They told him, "Jesus of Nazareth is passing by." And he cried, "Jesus, Son of David, have mercy on me!"* – Luke 18:35-39

FOR YEARS I sat by the side of the road that led to Jericho, relying on the kindness of strangers. As they passed by, some gave me something to eat, others a small shekel, but mostly, they ignored me as though I didn't exist. I am a human being, blind from birth. Because they thought that my blindness was the result of sin, they didn't want anything to do with me. I was like a leper.

When I sat by the side of the road, I heard a lot of what people were saying. I couldn't see, but I could hear. I heard their problems, their disputes, their fears and anxieties. I heard it all. In my head, I would solve their problems, settle their disagreements, and be their mighty champion, saving them from all that scared them.

They would probably be amazed by what goes on in the mind of a blind man. I might not have been able to see like everyone else, but I could see what they could not. Yet no one asked; no one came to me for advice.

I had an answer, but they never asked the question. I was blind. What did I matter?

I remember the day You and Your friends passed by. There was a commotion. There was excitement in the air. I could feel it. I tugged on someone's garment and asked who was passing by and they told me it was You. I had heard about You. Some spoke of You with amazement, talking about healings and wondrous works and a new teaching. Others thought You dangerous and not to be trusted. All I remember is that You were passing by and if You were who they said You were, You would notice me. You might even heal me so that I could see.

I began to shout, to cry out. I called Your name over and over. Some told me to be quiet; others kicked me and tried to push me out of the way.

What happened next I will never forget. You called me over and asked what I wanted You to do for me. I could hear Your voice, but I could not see Your face. Your voice was like no other that I had heard by the side of the road. There was compassion in Your voice — there was real concern. No one had ever spoken to me in that tone before. I was so enthralled by Your voice that I almost forgot what I wanted You to do.

Finally I said, "Lord, I want to see." No sooner did I say the words than the darkness in which I lived seemed to disappear. I was able to see. I was overwhelmed. I could see. And I remember thinking later that the first thing I saw was You, Your face. I saw You!

But now I am here on Calvary. I came because I heard what was happening to You. For the first time since You gave me sight, I wish I could not see. This is horrible. I can't believe what is before my eyes. I close them and turn away. I don't want to see. For the first time since You healed me, *I don't want to see.* Then in the darkness I hear You say, *"My God, My God, why have You forsaken Me?"*

I turn, with my eyes opened wide. You? You feel forsaken? I know that feeling. It brings me back to the roadside on the way to Jericho.

No, Jesus, You are not forsaken. I am here, Jesus, with my eyes wide open. I am here with You. You are not forsaken. I see You. I hear You. Jesus, it's me, the beggar. I'm here. Do You see *me*?

# The Lame Man
## at the Pool of Bethsaida

*John 5:2-16*

FROM THE GOSPEL ACCORDING TO ST. JOHN:

*Now there is in Jerusalem by the Sheep Gate
a pool, in Hebrew called Beth-za'tha,
which has five porticoes. In these lay a
multitude of invalids, blind, lame, paralyzed.
One man was there, who had been ill
for thirty-eight years. – John 5:2-5*

THERE ARE SO MANY PEOPLE HERE. Who are all these people? Are they like me? Are we all here because You changed our lives? Do You remember me, Jesus? I was the man by the side of the pool at Bethsaida here in Jerusalem. You came up to me and asked me if I wanted to be healed. I didn't know who You were. I began to tell You that despite sitting there for thirty-eight years, no one ever approached me to help me into the healing waters. They ignored me. No one cared. But You came up and asked if I wanted to be healed. You were the first person to ever pay attention to me, to offer assistance. I said yes, thinking that You were going to help put me in the water, but then something amazing happened.

I felt this strange sensation go through my legs. I haven't felt anything in my legs for thirty-eight years. Then You offered me Your hand and I stood up. For the first time in a long time, I stood up and I didn't fall. My legs were strong; they held me up.

These strong legs carried me here today. I heard what was happening to You. I had to come to be with You, Jesus. You who came to me; I needed to be with You. But now I hear You say, *"My God, My God, why have You forsaken Me?"* Those haunting words remind me of my years sitting by the pool of Bethsaida. Thirty-eight forsaken years. Thirty-eight years of no one paying any attention to me, only thinking of themselves. Your words pierce my heart and my memory.

After You healed me, I promised myself that I wouldn't let a day go by that I didn't extend some kindness to another person. Now, I am here on Calvary with You. You are not forsaken. I am here with You. You are not alone.

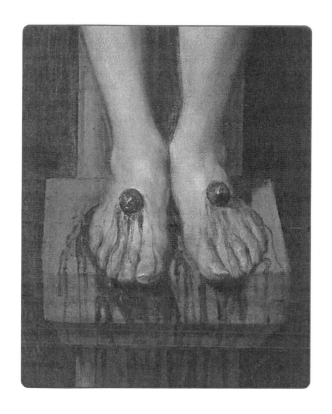

# THE FIFTH WORD

...Jesus, knowing that all was now finished, said (to fulfill the Scripture), **"I thirst."**

*John 19:28*

# The Woman at the Well

*John 4:7-24*

FROM THE GOSPEL ACCORDING TO ST. JOHN:

*[Jesus] left Judea and departed again to Galilee.
He had to pass through Samar'ia. So he came to a
city of Samar'ia, called Sy'char, near the field that
Jacob gave to his son Joseph. Jacob's well
was there, and so Jesus, wearied as he was
with his journey, sat down beside the well.
It was about the sixth hour.* – John 4:3-6

I CAME TO JERUSALEM FOR THE FEAST and I heard what they were doing to You. I had to come. I had to see You again. Little did I know when I sat with You at the well that I would one day be here beneath Your Cross. I hear You cry out, *"I thirst,"* and I cannot help but think of the time You said those very words to me.

You were thirsty. By all that is proper, You shouldn't have even spoken to me; yet You did. When I think back and replay our conversation over and over in my mind, I know now that it wasn't just a coincidence that we met at the well.

I was just going about my daily tasks, drawing the day's supply of water. I waited until the other women were gone, as I did every day. I hated the way they looked at me; their eyes felt like daggers piercing my heart.

It was better just to stay away than to endure their contempt. It was so hot, the sun bearing down at that hour of the day, but I really had no choice.

You spoke to me, You were kind to me, and I didn't know what to think, or what to say. No one really spoke to me. I always felt so lonely. But You spoke to me and all of those hurts and sorrows just came crashing down. You were thirsty and asked for a drink. I was so foolish to think that it was just because of the heat. Now I understand that it was much more.

That guard tried to give You something to drink, but I was not surprised that You didn't take it. I was so much like him before. I, too, handed You a cup of water, but that's not what You wanted then, just as that sponge is not what You want now.

I know now what You wanted and I've tried ever since our meeting at the well to give it to You. You want my heart, You want my love, You want my sins because they enslave my heart and lessen my love. That's what You thirst for.

It is so hard to see You like this. Your thirst for us is so great. Your concern for us, for what truly matters — that's what You thirst for and we don't understand it, we don't get it. But I know what You mean only because You took the time to sit with me at the well. My life has been so different since then, and I am so grateful to You. That is why I am here, even though it is so difficult to be here.

It is not only difficult for me. The young couple next to me is breaking my heart. They are inconsolable, holding each other so tightly and sobbing in each other's arms. You came to me when I didn't even think I needed You. It seems only right to reach out to them now. You comforted me; it is only right for me to comfort them.

# *The Newlyweds from Cana*

## *John 2:1-11*

FROM THE GOSPEL ACCORDING TO ST. JOHN:

> *On the third day there was a marriage*
> *at Cana in Galilee, and the mother*
> *of Jesus was there; Jesus also was invited*
> *to the marriage, with his disciples.*
>
> – John 2:1-2

WE WERE SO HONORED to have You and Your mother attend our wedding. We tried our best to make sure that our guests had an enjoyable time, as any young couple would. But the person in charge of supplying the wine was less than reliable. We found out that they ran out of wine soon after our celebration began. If it wasn't for You, Lord, we would have been very thirsty and very embarrassed. To hear You say that You thirst only makes this moment more painful in light of the memory of Your kindness to us on our wedding day.

We come to Jerusalem to celebrate the Passover every year; we have done so ever since we were married. Nowadays, we bring our children along with us. As we bless and drink the cup of wine during the Seder, we tell the story of what You did for us with the wine at our wedding. The story has become part of our ceremony.

Now You are thirsty and the only thing that we can give You in return is ourselves. We heard what was happening, and we risked the crowds, the guards, even the safety of our family, so that we could be with You in Your time of need—just as You were with us when we needed You.

We are all together here at the foot of Your Cross. We hold each other tight with tears streaming down our faces. We say nothing. We just cry. We hope that our tears and the tears of our children will quench Your thirst. We renew our promise to each other at the foot of Your Cross. We promise to be faithful. We promise to raise our children to love and serve God. It is our prayer that fulfilling our promises and living faithfully will quench Your thirst.

# The Sixth Word

It was now about the sixth hour, and there was darkness over the whole land until the ninth hour, while the sun's light failed; and the curtain of the temple was torn in two. Then Jesus, crying with a loud voice, said, "**Father, into your hands I commit my spirit!**" And having said this he breathed his last.

*Luke 23:44-46*

# The Woman with a Hemorrhage

*Mark 5:24b-34*

<small>FROM THE GOSPEL ACCORDING TO ST. MARK:</small>

*And a great crowd followed [Jesus]
and thronged about him. And there was
a woman who had had a flow of blood
for twelve years, and who had suffered much
under many physicians, and had spent
all that she had, and was no better
but rather grew worse.* – Mark 5:24b-26

FOR TWELVE YEARS, the flow of blood drained every ounce of my strength, my savings, my whole livelihood. I endured painful examinations from one physician after another. No one could help; no one could figure out what caused my problem. But it didn't stop them from taking my money. All of my savings was gone. I was at the point of being destitute. Worse than that, I was losing hope. I was giving up on my life. What life? I had no life, at least not one worth living. Despair — I was at the point of despair.

Wandering aimlessly through my village, my head in a daze, not knowing what to do, I suddenly found myself in the midst of a great crowd of people. I didn't know how I got there or what was going on. I gathered myself together enough to inquire what was happening and someone told me that You, Jesus, were there.

I remembered hearing about You from neighbors. They told me about Your teachings. They said that You healed the sick.

My thoughts were interrupted when I learned that You had received word about a little girl who was at the point of death and You were going to her. All of a sudden, I panicked. I thought that my last chance for being healed was standing right before me. It was You. And You were about to leave. I tried to think of what to do, but I was a mess. I couldn't think straight. All I knew was that my last hope was slipping away. You healed the sick. I was sick! You could heal me! What could I do?

There were too many people shouting at You, demanding Your attention. Then I thought, *Just touch His garment.* Just to touch Your clothing would be enough. You were my last hope. You were my only hope. You healed others... I knew that You would heal me.

I reached out my hand and brushed Your cloak. As my hand met Your garment, I could feel a wave of warmth across my body, a warmth I had never felt before, a warmth that penetrated the very core of my being.

Suddenly, my mind was clear, my heart was full, I felt strong again. I was aware that my flow of blood had stopped. There was no more pain, no more discomfort. I felt well. After twelve long years, I finally felt well.

Then You turned and asked, "Who touched Me?"

I became frightened. Did I do something wrong? Should I have asked You first? You kept looking around and asking who had touched You.

Finally, I came forward. I was trembling uncontrollably. I was filled with fear. I fell on the ground at Your feet and told You the whole truth about my life. You were so patient and, I will never forget this: You called me "daughter."

"Daughter," You said, "your faith has made you well. Go in peace, and be healed of your disease."

Faith was the only thing I had left and even that was small and near empty. I had not had peace in so long and You gave me that gift as well. And healing — after twelve long, agonizing years, there was finally healing.

Now I find myself in the midst of another crowd. I followed them up this hill to where You are hanging on this cross. Fear and trembling grip me once more. I fall on my knees before You, so great is my grief, and I want so desperately to touch You again. Then I hear You say, *"Father, into Your hands I commit My spirit!"*

Your words fill my heart and rekindle my memory. On the day You healed me, I gave myself over to You. You were my last hope. You were my only hope.

Now, helplessly nailed to the Cross, You give Yourself to Your Father in heaven. Your offering of self reminds me that when I had nothing left to give, You filled me with new life. I cannot help but think that in giving Yourself over to Your Father, He will restore You to the fullness of life.

Since You healed me, I even think differently. I see beyond the present moment and see something new, something fulfilled, something beautiful and full of life. I can think this way only because I gave myself to You, Jesus. You addressed me as daughter. I commit my spirit with Yours to our Father. I am here, Jesus, in Your time of need, just as You were there in my time. I am here, Jesus. You are not alone.

# THE SEVENTH WORD

A bowl full of vinegar stood there; so
they put a sponge full of the vinegar on
hyssop and held it to his mouth.
When Jesus had received the vinegar,
he said, **"It is finished."**

*John 19:29-30a*

# Lazarus, Martha, and Mary

## John 11:1-44

FROM THE GOSPEL ACCORDING TO ST. JOHN:

*Now a certain man was ill, Laz'arus of Beth'any,
the village of Mary and her sister Martha. It was Mary
who anointed the Lord with ointment and wiped his
feet with her hair, whose brother Laz'arus was ill.
So the sisters sent to him, saying, "Lord, he
whom you love is ill." But when Jesus heard it
he said, "This illness is not unto death; it is
for the glory of God, so that the Son of God
may be glorified by means of it."* – John 11:1-4

HOW OFTEN You visited our home. We were so honored that You found it to be a place to rest, far from the crowds that sought You out everywhere You went. That is what we wanted for You and Your friends: a quiet place to relax.

Now we find ourselves here beneath Your Cross. You mentioned this Cross time and again, but we never imagined the horror it would entail. It breaks our hearts standing here, seeing You like this, hearing You say, with such resignation, *"It is finished."* We can see that Your poor body is straining, Your breathing so labored. *"It is finished,"* You say — but we know deep down in our hearts that it is not finished.

When Lazarus was sick, we called for You, but it took so long for You to come to us. We lost our brother and even placed him in the tomb before You came to us. You cried with us; You comforted us with Your presence.

Then You finally made Your way to his tomb.

We were amazed, even horrified, that You asked that the stone be rolled away. We knew all too well the reality of death — its loss, its pain, its stench. But You spoke the word and our brother came forth, alive. To our utter amazement, he was alive! You told us to unbind him and then You gave him back to us. Knowing and believing with all our hearts that You have power over death, we cannot help but hear, *It is finished*, and we think, no, it is only beginning.

We thought Lazarus was finished, but You restored him to life, gave him back his human life; but he will die again. For You, however, it will be different. You are different. A new and more radiant life will come to be.

Gathered here beneath Your Cross, all of these people hear what we hear; but their experience is not what we experienced. They hear that it is over — done. Some think You a failure. They had placed all their hope in You and they now see You helpless and nailed to this Cross. It is finished in so many minds, but we know better. If You can restore our brother, what will the Father do for You and for us?

It is not finished; it is only the beginning — a new world, a new life. We believe this with all our hearts. Your love called Lazarus back to life.

Encountering You has stretched the yearning of our hearts. We dare to hope for more than we know — the unimaginable. Death has no permanence. Love is the power and light that destroys death's darkness. Your love has overcome death. You are Love's Light!

In You is all our hope.

*The author's childhood parish:*
*St. Mary's Church in Poughkeepsie, NY*

# REMEMBERING

EVERY SUNDAY DURING MY CHILDHOOD, my father would give me a quarter to light a candle in our parish church after Mass. I always chose to light my candle near the life-size crucifix which stood in the corner of the church.

After lighting my candle, I would kneel and recite the Prayer Before a Crucifix which was attached to the Cross just below Our Lord's feet. Then with childlike innocence, I would slowly lift my eyes to look at His face. The statue was designed so that Our Lord's eyes were still open. He would look at me and I would look at Him. I don't know how long I knelt there, but I remember having to be tapped on the shoulder to remind me that it was time to go.

Those moments of quietly looking into my Lord's eyes and He looking back into mine will remain poignant moments of grace that planted the seed of my vocation.

When St. Thomas Aquinas wrote his theological treatises, he did so before Our Lord crucified. It was beneath the Cross that all wisdom flowed, then as well as today. While Thomas was deep in prayer, Our Lord spoke to him: "You have written well of me, Thomas. What do you ask of me?"

"Only Yourself, Lord," Thomas responded. "Only Yourself."

## NOW GATHERED AT
## THE FOOT OF THE CROSS

D URING HIS PUBLIC MINISTRY, Jesus encountered many individuals, and their witness in Sacred Scripture powerfully changes our lives as well. Jesus continues to come to us. As He wills, we in turn make our own journey to the foot of His Cross. Only there do we hear Him speak to the very depths of our hearts. We come to console Him, to comfort Him, so that He may not be abandoned, nor forsaken, nor thirsty.

We are all looking to be loved. We all allow our possessions to possess us. We are all in need of healing and are at times dependent on the goodness of others. We are all sinners and in need of forgiveness, or are blind, or have some parts of us that are dead and need to be brought back to life. We are all gathered at the foot of His Cross. We come to hear Him, to look upon His face, and to console Him in His time of need because He has been so good to us. We come to be lifted up into His outstretched arms — to be transformed by His Love.

*We adore You, O Christ,*
*and we praise You.*
*Because by Your Holy Cross,*
*You have redeemed the world.*

†

# FOR FURTHER
# PRAYER AND REFLECTION

### PRAYERS   *54*
*selected by the author*

### SCRIPTURES   *65*
*featuring*
*the Gospel accounts cited*
*within the meditations*

# PRAYERS

## PRAYER BEFORE A CRUCIFIX

My good and dear Jesus,

I kneel before You, asking You most earnestly

to engrave upon my heart a deep and lively

faith, hope, and charity, with true repentance

for my sins, and a firm resolve to make amends.

As I reflect upon Your five wounds, and dwell

upon them with deep compassion and grief,

I recall, good Jesus, the words the prophet David

spoke long ago concerning Yourself:

*"They have pierced my hands and my feet;*

*they have counted all my bones."*

## ANIMA CHRISTI

Soul of Christ, make me holy.

Body of Christ, be my salvation.

Blood of Christ, let me drink Your wine.

Water flowing from the side of Christ, wash me clean.

Passion of Christ, strengthen me.

Kind Jesus, hear my prayer.

Hide me within Your wounds and keep me close to You.

Defend me from the evil enemy.

Call me at my death to the fellowship of Your saints,

that I may sing Your praise with them through all eternity.

Amen.

## SUSCIPE

Lord, Jesus Christ,

Take all my freedom, my memory,

my understanding, and my will.

All that I have and cherish You have given me.

I surrender it all to be guided by Your will.

Your grace and Your love are wealth enough for me.

Give me these, Lord Jesus, and I ask for nothing more.

Amen.

## ACT OF CONTRITION

O my God, I am heartily sorry
for having offended Thee, and I
detest all my sins because of Thy
just punishments, but most of all
because they offend Thee, my God,
who art all good and
deserving of all my love.
I firmly resolve with the help of
Thy grace to confess my sins,
to do penance, and to amend my life.
Amen.

## PRAYER TO OUR LADY OF SORROWS

*by St. Bonaventure*

O most holy Virgin, Mother of our Lord Jesus Christ, by the overwhelming grief you experienced when you witnessed the martyrdom, the crucifixion, and the death of your divine Son, look upon me with eyes of compassion, and awaken in my heart a tender commiseration for those sufferings, as well as a sincere detestation of my sins, in order that, being disengaged from all undue affection for the passing joys of this earth, I may long for the eternal Jerusalem, and that henceforth all my thoughts and all my actions may be directed towards this one most desirable object: Honor, glory, and love to our divine Lord Jesus, and to the holy and immaculate Mother of God.

Amen.

## FATIMA PRAYERS

### THE PARDON PRAYER

My God, I believe, I adore, I hope, and I love You!
I ask pardon for those who do not believe, do not
adore, do not hope, and do not love You!

### THE ANGEL'S PRAYER

O Most Holy Trinity, Father, Son, and Holy Spirit,
I adore You profoundly, and I offer You the most
precious Body, Blood, Soul, and Divinity of Jesus
Christ, present in all the tabernacles of the world,
in reparation for the outrages, sacrileges,
and indifference by which He is offended.
And, through the infinite merits of His Most
Sacred Heart and the Immaculate Heart of Mary,
I beg of You the conversion of poor sinners.
Amen.

### THE DECADE PRAYER

O my Jesus, forgive us our sins, save us from
the fires of hell. Lead all souls to heaven,
especially those in most need of Thy mercy.

*A Scriptural Rosary\* for the*

## Fifth Sorrowful Mystery
# THE CRUCIFIXION

*Begin the mystery by praying the*
OUR † FATHER

When they reached the place called The Skull,
they crucified him.
*Luke 23:33\*\**

*After each Scripture pray the*
HAIL † MARY

Jesus said, "Father, forgive them;
they do not know what they are doing."
*Luke 23:34*

HAIL † MARY

One of the criminals crucified with him said,
"Jesus, remember me when you come into your kingdom."
*Luke 23:39, 42; Mark 15:32*

HAIL † MARY

"Indeed, I promise you," he replied,
"today you will be with me in paradise."
*Luke 23:43*

HAIL † MARY

Near the cross of Jesus stood
his mother and the disciple he loved.
*John 19:25, 26*

HAIL † MARY

Jesus said to his mother, "Woman, this is your son."
Then to the disciple he said, "This is your mother."
*John 19:26, 27*

HAIL † MARY

And from that moment
the disciple made a place for her in his home.
*John 19:27*

HAIL † MARY

And a darkness came over the whole land,
and the earth quaked; and the veil
of the Temple was torn in two.
*Luke 23:44; Matthew 27:51*

HAIL + MARY

And Jesus cried out in a loud voice,
"Father, into your hands I commit my spirit."
*Luke 23:46*

HAIL † MARY

And bowing his head he breathed his last.
*John 19:30; Luke 23:46*

HAIL † MARY

*Conclude the mystery by praying:*

GLORY BE TO THE FATHER, AND TO THE SON,
AND TO THE HOLY SPIRIT. AS IT WAS IN THE BEGINNING,
IS NOW, AND EVER SHALL BE, WORLD WITHOUT END.
AMEN.

---

*With gratitude to John and Joanne Bolger for their lifetime of inspiration and encouragement in praying and promoting the Scriptural Rosary.

** Scriptures taken from the Jerusalem Bible. Copyright © 1966 by Darton, Longman and Todd, Ltd. and Doubleday and Co., Inc. Used by permission.

## STABAT MATER
*(Latin)*

Stabat Mater dolorosa
Iuxta Crucem lacrimosa,
Dum pendebat Filius.

Cuius animam gementem,
Contristatam et dolentem,
Pertransivit gladius.

O quam tristis et afflicta
Fuit illa benedicta
Mater Unigeniti!

Quem maerebat, et dolebat,
Pia Mater, dum videbat
Nati paenas inclyti.

Quis est homo, qui non fleret,
Matrem Christi si videret
In tanto supplicio?

Quis non posset contristari,
Christi Matrem contemplari
Dolentem cum Filio?

Pro peccatis suae gentis
Vidit Iesum in tormentis,
Et flagellis subditum.

Vidit suum dulcem natum
Moriendo desolatum,
Dum emisit spiritum.

Eia Mater, fons amoris,
Me sentire vim doloris
Fac, ut tecum lugeam.

Fac, ut ardeat cor meum
In amando Christum Deum,
Ut sibi complaceam.

## STABAT MATER
*(English)*

At the Cross her station keeping,
Stood the mournful Mother weeping,
Close to Jesus to the last.

Through her heart, His sorrow sharing,
All His bitter anguish bearing,
Now at length the sword had pass'd.

Oh, how sad and sore distress'd
Was that Mother highly blest
Of the sole-begotten One!

Christ above in torment hangs;
She beneath beholds the pangs
Of her dying, glorious Son.

Is there one who would not weep,
Whelmed in miseries so deep,
Christ's dear Mother to behold?

Can the human heart refrain
From partaking in her pain,
In that Mother's pain untold?

Bruised, derided, cursed, defiled,
She beheld her tender Child,
All with bloody scourges rent.

For the sins of His own nation
Saw Him hang in desolation
Till His spirit forth He sent.

O thou Mother! fount of love!
Touch my spirit from above;
Make my heart with thine accord.

Make me feel as thou hast felt;
Make my soul to glow and melt
With the love of Christ our Lord.

## STABAT MATER
### (Latin, cont'd)

Sancta Mater, istud agas,
Crucifixi fige plagas
Cordi meo valide.

Tui nati vulnerati,
Tam dignati pro me pati,
Paenas mecum divide.

Fac me tecum pie flere,
Crucifixo condolere,
Donec ego vixero.

**Iuxta Crucem tecum stare,**
Et me tibi sociare
In planctu desidero.

Virgo virginum praeclara,
Mihi iam non sis amara:
Fac me tecum plangere.

Fac, ut portem Christi mortem,
Passionis fac consortum,
Et plagas recolere.

Fac me plagis vulnerari,
Fac me Cruce inebriari,
Et cruore Filii.

Flammis ne urar succensus
Per te, Virgo, sim defensus
In die iudicii.

Christe, cum sit hinc exire,
Da per Matrem me venire
Ad palmam victoriae.

Quando corpus morietur,
Fac, ut animae donetur
Paradisi gloria. Amen. †

## STABAT MATER
### (English, cont'd)

Holy Mother! pierce me through;
In my heart each wound renew
Of my Savior crucified.

Let me share with thee His pain,
Who for all my sins was slain,
Who for me in torments died.

Let me mingle tears with thee,
Mourning Him who mourned for me,
All the days that I may live.

**Beneath the Cross with thee to stay,**
There with thee to weep and pray,
Is all I ask of thee to give.

Virgin of all virgins blest,
Listen to my fond request:
Let me share thy grief divine.

Let me, to my latest breath,
In my body bear the death
Of that dying Son of thine.

Wounded with His every wound,
Steep my soul till it hath swoon'd
In His very blood away.

Be to me, O Virgin, nigh,
Lest in flames I burn and die,
In His awful Judgment Day.

Christ, when Thou shalt call me hence,
Be Thy Mother my defense,
Be Thy Cross my victory.

While my body here decays,
May my soul Thy goodness praise,
Safe in Paradise with Thee. Amen. †

# SCRIPTURES

## The Woman Caught in Adultery

EARLY IN THE MORNING [Jesus] came again to the temple; all the people came to him, and he sat down and taught them. The scribes and the Pharisees brought a woman who had been caught in adultery, and placing her in their midst they said to him, "Teacher, this woman has been caught in the act of adultery. Now in the law Moses commanded us to stone such. What do you say about her?" This they said to test him, that they might have some charge to bring against him. Jesus bent down and wrote with his finger on the ground. And as they continued to ask him, he stood up and said to them, "Let him who is without sin among you be the first to throw a stone at her." And once more he bent down and wrote with his finger on the ground. But when they heard it, they went away, one by one, beginning with the eldest, and Jesus was left alone with the woman standing before him. Jesus looked up and said to her, "Woman, where are they? Has no one condemned you?" She said, "No one, Lord." And Jesus said, "Neither do I condemn you; go, and do not sin again."

John 8:2-11

## The Rich Young Man

AND BEHOLD, one came up to [Jesus], saying, "Teacher, what good deed must I do, to have eternal life?" And he said to him, "Why do you ask me about what is good? One there is who is good. If you would enter life, keep the commandments." He said to him, "Which?" And Jesus said, "You shall not kill, You shall not commit adultery, You shall not steal, You shall not bear false witness, Honor your father and mother, and, You shall love your neighbor as yourself." The young man said to him, "All these I have observed; what do I still lack?" Jesus said to him, "If you would be perfect, go, sell what you possess and give to the poor, and you will have treasure in heaven; and come, follow me." When the young man heard this he went away sorrowful; for he had great possessions.

Matthew 19:16-22

*The Paralytic Lowered from the Roof*

**Jesus Heals a Paralytic**

AND WHEN [JESUS] RETURNED to Caper'na-um after some days, it was reported that he was at home. And many were gathered together, so that there was no longer room for them, not even about the door; and he was preaching the word to them. And they came, bringing to him a paralytic carried by four men. And when they could not get near him because of the crowd, they removed the roof above him; and when they had made an opening, they let down the pallet on which the paralytic lay. And when Jesus saw their faith, he said to the paralytic, "Child, your sins are forgiven." Now some of the scribes were sitting there, questioning in their hearts, "Why does this man speak like this? It is blasphemy! Who can forgive sins but God alone?" And immediately Jesus, perceiving in his spirit that they questioned like this within themselves, said to them, "Why do you question like this in your hearts? Which is easier, to say to the paralytic, 'Your sins are forgiven,' or to say, 'Rise, take up your pallet and walk'? But that you may know that the Son of man has authority on earth to forgive sins" — he said to the paralytic — "I say to you, rise, take up your pallet and go home." And he rose, and immediately took up the pallet and went out before them all; so that they were all amazed and glorified God, saying, "We never saw anything like this!"

Mark 2:1-12

## The Raising of the Widow's Son

SOON AFTERWARD [Jesus] went to a city called Na'in, and his disciples and a great crowd went with him. As he drew near to the gate of the city, behold, a man who had died was being carried out, the only son of his mother, and she was a widow; and a large crowd from the city was with her. And when the Lord saw her, he had compassion on her and said to her, "Do not weep." And he came and touched the bier, and the bearers stood still. And he said, "Young man, I say to you, arise." And the dead man sat up, and began to speak. And he gave him to his mother. Fear seized them all; and they glorified God, saying, "A great prophet has arisen among us!" and "God has visited his people!" And this report concerning him spread through the whole of Judea and all the surrounding country.

Luke 7:11-17

## Our Lady's Meditation

AND WHEN THE TIME CAME for their purification according to the law of Moses, they brought him up to Jerusalem to present him to the Lord (as it is written in the law of the Lord, "Every male that opens the womb shall be called holy to the Lord") and to offer a sacrifice according to what is said in the law of the Lord, "a pair of turtledoves, or two young pigeons." Now there was a man in Jerusalem, whose name was Simeon, and this man was righteous and devout, looking for the consolation of Israel, and the Holy Spirit was upon him. And it had been revealed to him by the Holy Spirit that he should not see death before he had seen the Lord's Christ. And inspired by the Spirit he came into the temple; and when the parents brought in the child Jesus, to do for him according to the custom of the law, he took him up in his arms and blessed God and said, "Lord, now let your servant depart in peace, according to your word; for my eyes have seen your salvation which you have prepared in the presence of all peoples, a light for revelation to the Gentiles, and for glory to your people Israel."

And his father and his mother marveled at what was said about him; and Simeon blessed them and said to Mary his mother, "Behold, this child is set for the fall and rising of many in Israel, and for a sign that is spoken against (and a sword will pierce through your own soul also), that thoughts out of many hearts may be revealed."

And there was a prophetess, Anna, the daughter of Phan'uel, of the tribe of Asher; she was of a great age, having lived with her husband seven years from her virginity, and as a widow till she was eighty-four. She did not depart from the temple, worshiping with fasting and prayer night and day. And coming up at that very hour she gave thanks to God, and spoke of him to all who were looking for the redemption of Jerusalem.

**The Return to Nazareth**
And when they had performed everything according to the law of the Lord, they returned into Galilee, to their own city, Nazareth. And the child grew and became strong, filled with wisdom; and the favor of God was upon him.

Luke 2:22-40

## The Blind Man at the Side of the Road

As [JESUS] DREW NEAR to Jericho, a blind man was sitting by the roadside begging; and hearing a multitude going by, he inquired what this meant. They told him, "Jesus of Nazareth is passing by." And he cried, "Jesus, Son of David, have mercy on me!" And those who were in front rebuked him, telling him to be silent; but he cried out all the more, "Son of David, have mercy on me!" And Jesus stopped, and commanded him to be brought to him; and when he came near, he asked him, "What do you want me to do for you?" He said, "Lord, let me receive my sight." And Jesus said to him, "Receive your sight; your faith has made you well." And immediately he received his sight and followed him, glorifying God; and all the people, when they saw it, gave praise to God.

Luke 18:35-43

## The Lame Man at the Pool of Bethsaida

**Jesus Heals on the Sabbath**

NOW THERE IS IN JERUSALEM by the Sheep Gate a pool, in Hebrew called Beth-za'tha, which has five porticoes. In these lay a multitude of invalids, blind, lame, paralyzed. One man was there, who had been ill for thirty-eight years. When Jesus saw him and knew that he had been lying there a long time, he said to him, "Do you want to be healed?" The sick man answered him, "Sir, I have no man to put me into the pool when the water is troubled, and while I am going another steps down before me." Jesus said to him, "Rise, take up your pallet, and walk." And at once the man was healed, and he took up his pallet and walked.

Now that day was the sabbath. So the Jews said to the man who was cured, "It is the sabbath, it is not lawful for you to carry your pallet." But he answered them, "The man who healed me said to me, 'Take up your pallet, and walk.'" They asked him, "Who is the man who said to you, 'Take up your pallet, and walk'?" Now the man who had been healed did not know who it was, for Jesus had withdrawn, as there was a crowd in the place. Afterward, Jesus found him in the temple, and said to him, "See, you are well! Sin no more, that nothing worse befall you." The man went away and told the Jews that it was Jesus who had healed him. And this was why the Jews persecuted Jesus, because he did this on the sabbath.

John 5:2-16

## The Woman at the Well

THERE CAME A WOMAN of Samar'ia to draw water. Jesus said to her, "Give me a drink." For his disciples had gone away into the city to buy food. The Samaritan woman said to him, "How is it that you, a Jew, ask a drink of me, a woman of Samar'ia?" For Jews have no dealings with Samaritans. Jesus answered her, "If you knew the gift of God, and who it is that is saying to you, 'Give me a drink,' you would have asked him and he would have given you living water." The woman said to him, "Sir, you have nothing to draw with, and the well is deep; where do you get that living water? Are you greater than our father Jacob, who gave us the well, and drank from it himself, and his sons, and his cattle?" Jesus said to her, "Every one who drinks of this water will thirst again, but whoever drinks of the water that I shall give him will never thirst; the water that I shall give him will become in him a spring of water welling up to eternal life." The woman said to him, "Sir, give me this water, that I may not thirst, nor come here to draw."

Jesus said to her, "Go, call your husband, and come here." The woman answered him, "I have no husband." Jesus said to her, "You are right in saying, 'I have no husband'; for you have had five husbands, and he whom you now have is not your husband; this you said truly." The woman said to him, "Sir, I perceive that you are a prophet. Our fathers worshiped on this mountain; and you say that in Jerusalem is the place where men ought to worship." Jesus said to her, "Woman, believe me, the hour is coming when neither on this mountain nor in Jerusalem will you worship the Father. You worship what you do not know; we worship what we know, for salvation is from the Jews. But the hour is coming, and now is, when the true worshipers will worship the Father in spirit and truth, for such the Father seeks to worship him. God is spirit, and those who worship him must worship in spirit and truth."

John 4:7-24

## The Newlyweds from Cana

ON THE THIRD DAY there was a marriage at Cana in Galilee, and the mother of Jesus was there; Jesus also was invited to the marriage, with his disciples. When the wine failed, the mother of Jesus said to him, "They have no wine." And Jesus said to her, "O woman, what have you to do with me? My hour has not yet come." His mother said to the servants, "Do whatever he tells you." Now six stone jars were standing there, for the Jewish rites of purification, each holding twenty or thirty gallons. Jesus said to them, "Fill the jars with water." And they filled them up to the brim. He said to them, "Now draw some out, and take it to the steward of the feast." So they took it. When the steward of the feast tasted the water now become wine, and did not know where it came from (though the servants who had drawn the water knew), the steward of the feast called the bridegroom and said to him, "Every man serves the good wine first; and when men have drunk freely, then the poor wine; but you have kept the good wine until now." This, the first of his signs, Jesus did at Cana in Galilee, and manifested his glory; and his disciples believed in him.

John 2:1-11

## The Woman with a Hemorrhage

AND A GREAT CROWD FOLLOWED [JESUS] and thronged about him. And there was a woman who had had a flow of blood for twelve years, and who had suffered much under many physicians, and had spent all that she had, and was no better but rather grew worse. She had heard the reports about Jesus, and came up behind him in the crowd and touched his garment. For she said, "If I touch even his garments, I shall be made well." And immediately the hemorrhage ceased; and she felt in her body that she was healed of her disease. And Jesus, perceiving in himself that power had gone forth from him, immediately turned about in the crowd, and said, "Who touched my garments?" And his disciples said to him, "You see the crowd pressing around you, and yet you say, 'Who touched me?'" And he looked around to see who had done it. But the woman, knowing what had been done to her, came in fear and trembling and fell down before him, and told him the whole truth. And he said to her, "Daughter, your faith has made you well; go in peace, and be healed of your disease."

Mark 5:24b-34

## Lazarus, Martha, and Mary

### The Death of Lazarus

NOW A CERTAIN MAN WAS ILL, Laz'arus of Beth'any, the village of Mary and her sister Martha. It was Mary who anointed the Lord with ointment and wiped his feet with her hair, whose brother Laz'arus was ill. So the sisters sent to him, saying, "Lord, he whom you love is ill." But when Jesus heard it he said, "This illness is not unto death; it is for the glory of God, so that the Son of God may be glorified by means of it."

Now Jesus loved Martha and her sister and Laz'arus. So when he heard that he was ill, he stayed two days longer in the place where he was. Then after this he said to the disciples, "Let us go into Judea again." The disciples said to him, "Rabbi, the Jews were but now seeking to stone you, and are you going there again?" Jesus answered, "Are there not twelve hours in the day? If any one walks in the day, he does not stumble, because he sees the light of this world. But if any one walks in the night, he stumbles, because the light is not in him." Thus he spoke, and then he said to them, "Our friend Laz'arus has fallen asleep, but I go to awake him out of sleep." The disciples said to him, "Lord, if he has fallen asleep, he will recover." Now Jesus had spoken of his death, but they thought that he meant taking rest in sleep. Then Jesus told them plainly, "Laz'arus is dead; and for your sake I am glad that I was not there, so that you may believe. But let us go to him." Thomas, called the Twin, said to his fellow disciples, "Let us also go, that we may die with him."

### Jesus the Resurrection and the Life

Now when Jesus came, he found that Laz'arus had already been in the tomb four days. Beth'any was near Jerusalem, about two miles off, and many of the Jews had come to Martha and Mary to console them concerning their brother. When Martha heard that Jesus was coming, she went and met him, while Mary sat in the house. Martha said to Jesus, "Lord, if you had been here, my brother would not have died. And even now I know that whatever you ask from God, God will give you." Jesus said to her, "Your brother will rise again." Martha

*continued on next page*

*continued from previous page*

said to him, "I know that he will rise again in the resurrection at the last day." Jesus said to her, "I am the resurrection and the life; he who believes in me, though he die, yet shall he live, and whoever lives and believes in me shall never die. Do you believe this?" She said to him, "Yes, Lord; I believe that you are the Christ, the Son of God, he who is coming into the world."

### Jesus Weeps

When she had said this, she went and called her sister Mary, saying quietly, "The Teacher is here and is calling for you." And when she heard it, she rose quickly and went to him. Now Jesus had not yet come to the village, but was still in the place where Martha had met him. When the Jews who were with her in the house, consoling her, saw Mary rise quickly and go out, they followed her, supposing that she was going to the tomb to weep there. Then Mary, when she came where Jesus was and saw him, fell at his feet, saying to him, "Lord, if you had been here, my brother would not have died." When Jesus saw her weeping, and the Jews who came with her also weeping, he was deeply moved in spirit and troubled; and

he said, "Where have you laid him?" They said to him, "Lord, come and see." Jesus wept. So the Jews said, "See how he loved him!" But some of them said, "Could not he who opened the eyes of the blind man have kept this man from dying?"

### Jesus Raises Lazarus to Life

Then Jesus, deeply moved again, came to the tomb; it was a cave, and a stone lay upon it. Jesus said, "Take away the stone." Martha, the sister of the dead man, said to him, "Lord, by this time there will be an odor, for he has been dead four days." Jesus said to her, "Did I not tell you that if you would believe you would see the glory of God?" So they took away the stone. And Jesus lifted up his eyes and said, "Father, I thank you that you have heard me. I knew that you always hear me, but I have said this on account of the people standing by, that they may believe that you sent me." When he had said this, he cried with a loud voice, "Laz'arus, come out." The dead man came out, his hands and feet bound with bandages, and his face wrapped with a cloth. Jesus said to them, "Unbind him, and let him go."

John 11:1-44

# ILLUSTRATION CREDITS

Cover, page 49, and details on pages 26, 35, 41: *Cristo Crucificado (Christ Crucified)* by Diego Velázquez, 1632. Museo del Prado. Public domain.

Dedication, page 5: *Our Lady of Sorrows* by Linda Colacicco. Copyright © 2020. Used by permission of the artist.

Page 6: *Pietà* in St. Patrick's Cathedral, sculpted by William Ordway Partridge in 1906. Courtesy of St. Patrick's Cathedral.

Pages 10, 53 and 64: Original wood carvings from the sanctuary of St. Joseph's Church in Millbrook, NY. These three images, symbols of Our Lord's Passion, have been provided with the gracious assistance of Fr. Hartley Bancroft and photographed by Leigh Knickerbocker.

Foreword, page 12: Timothy Cardinal Dolan, 2020. Courtesy of St. Patrick's Cathedral. Copyright © 2020.

Page 29: Wooden crucifix at St. Joseph's Church in Millbrook, NY. Photographed by Joseph Sinnott.

Page 50: Archival photo of St. Mary's Church in Poughkeepsie, NY. Courtesy of Fr. Ronald Perez.

Back cover: The author at St. Patrick's Cathedral on Good Friday 2020. Courtesy of St. Patrick's Cathedral. Copyright © 2020.

# ACKNOWLEDGMENTS

IT IS WITH DEEP GRATITUDE that I acknowledge the gift of God made present through the following people:

My parents, for the gift of life and for passing on the faith.

His Eminence, Timothy Michael Cardinal Dolan, for extending the invitation to preach these meditations and for his generous words in the Foreword.

The Reverend Monsignor Robert Ritchie, for his graciousness in welcoming me into the pulpit of St. Patrick's Cathedral.

Sister Marie Pappas, CR, for her encouragement and guidance.

Leigh Knickerbocker, Andrea Serra, and Timothy and Yvonne Walsh, for their generosity of time and talent in reviewing and proofreading.

Joseph Sinnott for his patience and direction through the publishing process.

My sister, Linda, for her beautiful painting of Our Lady of Sorrows.

And all those who viewed these meditations on the website of St. Patrick's Cathedral and on YouTube, offering such kind and generous comments — and those who will pray beneath the Cross.

*God bless you all.*

## ABOUT THE AUTHOR

THE MOST REVEREND GERARDO J. COLACICCO is an Auxiliary Bishop of the Archdiocese of New York, consecrated on the feast of Our Lady of Loreto, December 10, 2019, at St. Patrick's Cathedral. His Episcopal motto is "Credo" ("I believe").

He was invited by Cardinal Dolan to preach the Seven Last Words in St. Patrick's Cathedral on Good Friday 2020. The cathedral was empty but the meditations were livestreamed and viewed by many.

Bishop Colacicco attended St. Joseph's Seminary, Dunwoodie in Yonkers, New York, and was ordained a priest in 1982. He has a licentiate in canon law from the Pontifical University of St. Thomas Aquinas Angelicum in Rome.

The Bishop has served in a number of parishes, as well as special assignments at the Seminary and on the Metropolitan Tribunal. He is at heart a parish priest and was honored to be pastor of the following parishes: Sacred Heart, Newburgh; St. Columba, Hopewell Junction; and St. Joseph – Immaculate Conception, Millbrook — all in the Archdiocese of New York.

A Fourth Degree member of the Knights of Columbus, the Bishop is an Associate Chaplain for the New York State Council. Presently, he is the Episcopal Vicar for the northern counties of the Archdiocese of New York, which include Dutchess, Orange, Ulster, and Sullivan counties.

*To contact the author, please send email to:*
beneaththecross7@gmail.com